WILD SOUTHLANDS

Photography by Bates Littlehales ❧ *Introduction by Michael Godfrey*

THOMASSON-GRANT
Charlottesville, Virginia

Published by Thomasson-Grant, Inc.
Designed by Gibson Parsons Design
Edited by Rebecca Beall Barns and Owen Andrews

Printed and bound in Singapore by Khai Wah Litho Pte. Ltd.

97 96 95 94 93 92 91 90   5 4 3 2 1

Any inquiries should be directed to Thomasson-Grant, Inc.
One Morton Drive, Suite 500, Charlottesville, Virginia 22901
(804) 977-1780

Library of Congress Cataloging-in-Publication Data
Littlehales, Bates.
    Wild southlands / photography by Bates Littlehales : introduction
by Michael Godfrey.
       p.   cm.
    Includes bibliographical references.
    ISBN 0-934738-58-0
    1. Natural history – Southern States.   2. Natural history – Southern
States – Pictorial works.   I. Title.
QH104.5.S59L57   1990
508.75 – dc20   90-10850
                                                              CIP

THOMASSON-GRANT

Male tiger swallowtail on firewheel, Virginia. 🦋 5

PAPILIO GLAUCUS; GAILLARDIA *SP.*

WE DREAM OF A LAND untouched by any hand save that of the Maker. It is a land of towering trees and dappled glades. The air here is innocent of the ring of the axe, the flatulence of the diesel. This is our special, unchanging, uncorrupted Eden, seat of tribal memory.

Hudson River painters aside, the land of untainted maturity, of dark, vast forests canopied 50 fathoms over by mega-oaks and hyper-hickories, has not existed in eastern North America since the weight of the ice lifted. It may never have existed. The Hudson River painters, according to an errant—though emerging—view of the North American land, documented a romance. Church and Bierstadt painted an arborscape of the spirit, knowing how strongly we respond to that vision of how wonderful the world would be without us—without us, but just before us, ripe and waiting, that we may have our way.

By any account, we've had our way with North America, and a few other continents as well. The "we," though, of this excess may be all of the cultures which have occupied North America over the span of human history. For a thousand generations, we have held sway here, and the evidence suggests that, dress us in hunter's skins or realtor's polyester, we feel compelled to alter the landscape.

In 1539, the aureatrophic Spanish under De Soto marched out of Florida to sniff the Carolinas for gold. During a day's march on June 2, 1540, the force of 300 soldiers and 500 horses passed through six villages before camping on open ground near what is now Asheville. One village provided 500 bearers to shoulder De Soto's baggage, evidence of a large, organized native population in western North Carolina. Subsistence hunting could not have supported so many populous settlements.

Cruising the coast of the Carolinas with Sir Francis Drake in 1586, a diarist wrote that the expedition was never out of sight of smoke, noting "one special great fire, which was very ordinary alongst this coast." The pall darkening Drake's sky suggests more than occasional slash-and-burn gestures for garden clearings.

(Facing) Hardwood forest, &c 7
John James Audubon State Park, Kentucky.

The land was being systematically maintained for growing crops and grazing animals—bison, likely, but also deer, turkeys, quail, and a dozen other edibles which thrive along the edges and in open places.

Not long after Jamestown was founded in 1607, the celebrated John Smith of that settlement spent time as an involuntary guest of a nearby Indian tribe. In his meticulous reports, Smith described a vigorous people in full use and occupancy of their land. He wrote, "The greatest labour they take, is in planting their corne, for the Country naturally is overgrowne with wood. To prepare the ground, they bruise the barke of the trees neare the root, then doe they scorch with fire that they grow no more .... Their houses are in the midst of their fields or gardens ... some 20 acres, some 40, some 100, some 200, some more, some lesse. Neare their habitations is little small wood or old trees ... by reason of their burning of them ...."

Early traders trekking south out of Virginia to do business with the Catawba and the Waxhaw found large tracts of the central Piedmont smoothed in grasslands. References like "Haw Fields" and "Buffalo Creek" appearing on the earliest maps of North Carolina hint that Indians maintained grasslands for grazing animals.

Forestry historians now suggest that most of deciduous North America has been in a cycle of clearing and abandonment for thousands of years. Native Americans apparently cycled the land through clearing, cultivation, abandonment, reforestation, then clearing again about every 200 years. Moreover, major hurricanes strike the coasts of North America every 50 years or so, and the trees most vulnerable to the ripping gales are the top-heavy giants whose accumulated mass gives leverage to the wind. As a result of human and other agencies, mature deciduous forest

8 🦃 *Wild turkey, Louisiana.*

MELEAGRIS GALLOPAVO

(Facing) Canada geese, Maryland.

BRANTA CANADENSIS

tracts dominated by very large hardwoods are un-likely to persist. Disease, storms, lightning, and flint-fingering bipeds have been historical constants. The permanent, stable forest is more myth than fact, and was so even in pre-Columbian times.

European man arrived and accelerated the defor-estation. It might be equally valid to say he shortened the cycle's length, for in spite of a national conceit termed "Manifest Destiny," there have been fallow periods for most parcels. The westward march brought new land under the axe, but also left behind abandoned fields.

If Indians, hurricanes, and bulldozers have been at work for so long felling forests in eastern North America, where does the tally stand? Broadly—and allowing for local variation—forests cover 70 percent, open lands 30 percent. That's a guess. A glance out your window from 33,000 feet en route from New York to Atlanta tells the tale. Clearly, eastern North America wants to be wooded, to be what biologists have long called it—the Eastern Deciduous Forest. The soils are good. Each year 40 to 60 inches of rain fall, and the sun shines for 240 days. To check the forest under those conditions requires an extravagant use of energy.

The force creating forests in eastern North America is called plant succession. Starting with abandoned farmland, a loosely predictable series of plant communities will cloak the landscape in a given place, one succeeding another, until a stable, but temporary, climax forest thrives. Unlike residents of the heaths of Scotland or the short-grass prairies of Wyoming, we in eastern North America cannot

10 🦋 *American mountain ash and red spruce,*
Dolly Sods Wilderness Area, West Virginia.
SORBUS AMERICANA; PICEA RUBENS

count on the fields of our youth to be the sods which will cover us. If they are, it's because somebody labored to keep them that way, mowing, cultivating, and grubbing to stay a step ahead of succession. In the Adirondacks, the old field-to-climax forest cycle time is perhaps 250 years. In Piedmont Georgia, it is less than half that.

In viewing the land as either tame or wild, we are speaking about plant succession—especially about the *rate* of succession. In North America, the rate is fastest in the Southeast. If the South can be said to have more than its share of wild places, that is because it can regenerate them more quickly when it loses them.

In the two centuries following Drake's voyage, the South was overrun with farmers of European extraction, and lost most of its wild places. Around Charleston, South Carolina, African slaves dug and winched great cypress stumps out of the swamp forests to make rice fields. Inland on the Coastal Plain, the work was no doubt easier, as the Indians had

probably kept much of the land open or in a state of arrested succession. Farther inland, the Piedmont's rolling, dissected curves came under the plow by the middle of the 18th century, and the deforesters pushed westward to Appalachia where they even tilled 60-degree slopes. By the middle of the 19th century, probably 70 percent of the South was under prosperous cultivation.

The good times did not last. The South was consumed in the most ghastly war in America's history, the first of the so-called "modern" wars in which economic destruction is integral. The region careened from plenty to penury, and its people spent the succeeding decades grubbing feebly in overgrown fields that were recently tall with cotton and corn.

Red spruce sapling, West Virginia. ❧ 11
PICEA RUBENS

IN THE SANDHILLS region along the southern margin of the Piedmont, sandy and somewhat poor soils feather onto low rises, and longleaf pine dominates the fire-arrested climax plant scheme. Planters long neglected the area, probably because, as in forests on poor soils everywhere, most of the nutrients are contained within the standing crop. The standing crop was magnificent—millions of acres of mature longleaf pine forest. It did not escape the notice of a Union cavalry officer, one John W. Roper of Philadelphia, who at war's end set about to unburden the Sandhills of the longleaf. He removed the timber, often, legend says, by confiscation under the occupation regime, the locals being in no position to protest.

Major Roper and others who saw the region's natural resources as ripe for the application of a little capital and technology were quite thorough. In the Sandhills, the surviving legacy of old-growth longleaf pine and wiregrass is confined to two small tracts preserved by The Nature Conservancy in the 1970s.

12 ❧ *Slash pines, Florida.*
PINUS ELLIOTTII

The longleaf/wiregrass association—like the great prairie grasslands of the West—is fire dependent. In the absence of regular fires, other vegetation takes over. Managed burning at The Nature Conservancy's Weymouth Woods Preserve in Southern Pines, North Carolina, keeps old-growth longleaf pine in dominance over wiregrass and scrubby turkey oaks. The burning minimizes fuel buildup and arrests the oaks' growth before they can muscle out the young pines. The pine seedlings somehow survive their introductory incinerations, and as the trees grow, their bark thickens to shield them against the fires to come.

A result of the burning is that there is little standing deadwood in the longleaf pine forests. The bark plates which guard veteran trees against fire slough off when the tree dies, leaving it to be consumed in the next blaze. Without deadwood, there are no woodpecker holes, and consequently no shelters for woodpeckers, screech owls, chickadees, titmice, crested flycatchers, bluebirds, flickers, gray squirrels, flying squirrels, honeybees, or any other cavity-nesting creature. In deciduous forests, half a dozen different woodpeckers can drill holes in the persistent standing deadwood. In the Sandhills, only one woodsman can hammer into the hard, resinous trunk of the living longleaf: the red-cockaded woodpecker, a rare bird indeed.

Jay Carter of Southern Pines, an authority on red-cockaded woodpeckers, has found that it takes the birds several years to excavate cavities in the living longleaf. Communal nesters, they create a cluster of holes in nearby trees in which they nest in season and roost every night. A night outside a roosting cavity—say, when a colony's stand is clear-cut—puts the red-cockaded woodpecker into the screech owl's gullet.

The Weymouth Woods Preserve and the stands on the nearby Fort Bragg Army Reservation are among the world's few longleaf pine/red-cockaded woodpecker communities. Among the "cockades," feeding is a joint effort. Parents and uncles and pals all forage to bring off a brood every spring. They in turn will spend their lives drilling on behalf of the bluebirds and small mammals which make up the community. Wild? Priceless might be a better term.

A BACKROADS JOURNEY south from New York or Philadelphia reveals a regional contrast in the way people view their land and, by inference, themselves. Farm country in southeastern Pennsylvania, Amish and secular alike, shows a fixation on the condition of the land, the Piedmont quilting of cornfields, pastures, and neat woodlots. Fencerows are clean (not necessarily to the delight of wildlife), barns are statements in architecture, houses are painted. Distelfinks wink.

Through Maryland on Route 15 and into Northern Virginia, the groomed fields swell against the Catoctin Ridge's east flank, and banked barns are anchored with sides of stone sweated from the soil when Washington was a lad. The great estates pass—Ludwell (son of Lighthorse Harry) Lee's Belmont, George Carter's Oatlands, and James Monroe's seat at Oak Hill.

Fifty miles south of Washington, D.C., the Rapidan River marks the northern frontier of the South's abandoned farmland. During the Civil War, the Eastern armies spent months glaring at one another across the Rapidan, though pickets waded the stream for card games and barter. A drastic change in the landscape begins at about the Rapidan today. Indifference to the land sets in.

Two depressions stunned the South between the Civil War and the turn of the century. Each put some farmers out of business and weakened others. The Great Depression delivered the coup de grâce in 1929. In the 1930s, a malnourished population of subsistence farmers, black and white, fled the land en masse, relinquishing, at an unprecedented rate, the stewardship of their gullied fields to plant succession.

The region never recovered from the Great Depression, and in terms of wild places we might hope it never does.

For the next 600 miles southbound, you are in the realm of plant succession. Though the process is at work just about everywhere in North America, in the South since the 1930s, it has been in control.

Succession really begins not when a field is abandoned, but when it is plowed for corn. As the corn germinates, so do grasses and asters whose seeds have been dropped by birds and wind. If the corn isn't plowed between the rows, the asters will take over during the growing season.

After harvest, the recently bare ground is matted with rosettes of asters, winter annuals which bide the cold months and build roots to steal a march on other opportunists when the days again lengthen. If the field isn't plowed the following year, the asters leap for the sunlight by the summer solstice, overtopping the crabgrass and even a tall man, should one venture nostalgically into the tangle.

Then comes broomsedge—not a sedge, really, but a grass which grows in aggressive, spreading tussocks. By the end of the third year after cultivation, the broomsedge tussocks have met and claimed the cornfield, waving rusty plumage at the winter wind.

Pines are among the few plants which can germinate in the broomsedge rootmat. Fields of broomsedge dotted with pine seedlings are a signature of succession in the Piedmont and much of the southern Atlantic Coastal Plain, though they prevail

Red-legged locust, Maryland. 𝕒 15
MELANOPLUS FEMUR-RUBRUM

less now as the abandoned fields of earlier decades progress into advanced stages.

Within a decade, the pines (or eastern red cedar on some fields, especially in Maryland and Virginia) close ranks to form a canopy. Fifteen years after the

plow in the southern Piedmont and Coastal Plain, we stand in a forest.

Pines completely dominate for two or three decades, shedding their lower branches as they stretch for the sun. Spiking skyward at 35 years, almost too big for a sap-sticky hug, the loblolly pine is the most

valuable lawful vegetation the region produces. Marketed under the rubric "southern yellow pine," loblolly, together with shortleaf and Virginia, is easily the continent's best structural lumber. The Northwest's cheaper and more popular true cedar lumber is brittle and twist-prone by comparison.

Because the pine phase of a forest is the only phase of significant commercial value and because depression-era abandonment threw much of the South into pinelands, any natural threat such as fire or the pine bark beetle draws yowls. To the farmer of modest means—not a rarity in the South—a growing pine stand is a savings account. It can be cashed in at a convenient time, or when the sweating banker visits.

Typically, pines are cut and sold at about 30 years, expediting the next successional phase. Young pines don't germinate under mature pines, but several important deciduous pioneers do—especially sweet gum, red maple, and tulip poplar. When pines are cut, an understory of bent pioneer hardwoods remains. If the pines aren't cut, they die anyway within

16 ❧ *White-throated sparrow, Maryland.*
ZONOTRICHIA ALBICOLLIS

the next few decades, as sweet gums and tulip poplars, genetically prepared to climb higher than pines, take the canopy. Taking the canopy is important because it gives first crack at the sun. Living in a neighbor's shadow is not a tree's formula for success.

Pines in the South are by nature transitory, the first woody plants on the soil after abandonment or disturbance. Fifty years is a long time for a pine to stand. For all except the longleaf, 75 years is exceptional. The term virgin cannot accurately be applied to Southern pines; something had to happen to their predecessor forest for the pines to get started. They are simply a step in the successional march.

Pine seeds have a flaky-margined case which helps them float on the wind, though they can as easily travel in the bowel of a bird. Deciduous pioneers are also breeze- or bird-transported. The spiraling bees' wings which bemuse us as children turn out to be the seeds of the red maple encased in an airfoil. The tulip tree's seed, twirling on a winglike bract, can make respectable way on a stiff wind. Sweet gum seeds are best moved by high-feeding forest fringillids such as American goldfinches, purple finches, and evening grosbeaks.

The pioneers share one trait: their seeds arrive without the help of squirrels. Squirrels are reluctant  residents in pine stands, probably for the same reason people don't enjoy climbing pines—it takes forever to get the sticky resins off. And pines don't offer many cavities within, so any shelter must be built; twigs must be cut and carried at the expense of gumming up one's whiskers.

Ah, but maples and gums and tulip poplars make admirable squirrel quarters. For a while, the squirrels seem content on a mush of poplar cones and maple buds. In time, though, they long to kerf hard-coated nuts. Squirrels will go any distance to collect acorns

Blue jay, Florida. ❧ 17
CYANOCITTA CRISTATA

and hickory nuts which they sequester in the duff under deciduous trees. Indefatigable hiders, indifferent finders, they quickly populate the forest with the oaks and hickories which will in time claim the canopy. When this happens, the southern forest is said to be at climax. That is, in the absence of disturbance, the oak-hickory stands replace themselves with similar stands. Disturbance being a near certainty, however, this seral state is set back from time to time.

IN THE SOUTH, we look for wild places in our own tracks, for our tracks are everywhere. Virtually 100 percent of the arable land has been culti-

vated, or at least pastured, since European man arrived, and probably for millennia before that. In this highly manipulated landscape, the wildness we find is a child of accommodation. Passenger pigeons, red wolves, Carolina parakeets, and ivory-billed woodpeckers could not accommodate our tamperings. White-tailed deer, opossums, and mockingbirds could, and have prospered. To survive in the South, one must adapt to abrupt change, regardless of leg-count.

If our tracks are everywhere, many of them are now overgrown. In a century, the region's balance has swung from two-thirds open land to two-thirds woodland. The departing traveller's first view after clearing the treetops at Raleigh-Durham Airport is of lush green fingering into Durham, Chapel Hill, and Raleigh. Only the centers of the towns poke through the canopy. Although the region has grown at a cancerous rate in the last 20 years, our clawings at the land are scarcely visible under the parasol of pines. Neon and pavement line the arteries, as throughout

Northern mockingbird, Maryland.
MIMUS POLYGLOTTOS

the cultural monolith we have created in North America, but the pines creep into and over the asphalt—Walker Percy's kudzu tendrils, probing for lax vigilance. Let the boom pass, and the pines will press the advantage.

Having usurped the land from Native Americans, European man has disenfranchised himself from it. Few of us pick our own apples—though we could if that were our way—and even far from suburbia we wake to road noise, not roosters. The newly arrived among us have no sense of place yet. Refugees from Kenosha and Newark, we have come south with our employers because the taxes are lower and the locals still work with some sense of purpose. We are on the land, but no longer are we of it. A political manifesto prepared in the 1990s will not likely bear a signature like "John Carroll of Carrollton."

Nowhere other than the place of our childhood ever quite becomes home, and more often than not we long to return. We usually do so, even if wearing a smile affixed by the embalmer. Raised in the South,

one is forever hostage to a very strong sense of place. A Ferrari on a freeway does not compensate for the smell of a Georgia thunderstorm.

BY THE TIME SHERMAN got to Camden, South Carolina, his wrath was spent. The arson his men had raised to an art form on their way from Atlanta to Columbia had palled. Sherman torched the obligatory railroad station, courthouse, and library, but left ranks of antebellum homes. If you were born in Camden, no one would think you narrow if, after suitable travel, you chose to live there. You are the first of five generations offered the option of a decent living in the Southern town you were raised in. You may toil in any of the newly arrived industries, operate a bed-and-breakfast for the free-spending horsey

Raccoons, Florida. 🐾 19
PROCYON LOTOR

folk, or set up a direct-response marketing operation and enjoy fingertip access to every mode of international communication. Circumstance no longer obliges the Southerner to abandon his sense of place.  It merely inclines him to abandon his land as a source of sustenance.

Sadly, we only protect what we know and love. Away from the land we lose our sense of stewardship. Each year, we serve a slice of land we have abandoned to developers who, having rendered northern New Jersey nearly uninhabitable, now follow Major Roper south. Or north, for Dallas finances much of the new abuse. Skinned of rootmat, topsoil, and saprolite, the lands we "develop" (an absurd misuse of the language) are lost to us. Paved over, the land is dead—out of the ferment of life. The earth might as well have shrunk by the acreage of each new shopping center.

Urban sprawl is the most visible sore on the South today. Starved for a century, we don't care to temper the feast with concern over acres we never gave a toot about anyway. "Hey, land, that's something the county makes you pay taxes on, then the banker takes away from you." If insurance companies and foreigners buy up a few hundred thousand acres of Coastal Plain pocosins and convert them into pesticide-soaked megafarms, should we let the resulting destruction of the Pamlico Sound estuaries and the North Carolina commercial fishing industry stay progress? Agricultural abuse, even on a grand scale, is among the less visible lesions on the land. Be thankful, we are told, that we didn't inherit a sheet of coal a hundred miles on a side just beneath an "overburden" of life-bearing soil, like West Virginia or southeastern Ohio.

In the 1940s and 50s, northern Virginia was rural. Winchester, population 18,000, was a big town. To

20 ❧ *Swamp rabbit, Louisiana.*
SYLVILAGUS AQUATICUS

the east, the Potomac contained Washington, vast and alien. Everyone farmed during the week and came to the fairs and livestock sales in Leesburg and Purcellville and Warrenton on Saturdays. Prosperity took the form of bulldozing a stand or two of locust and ailanthus off pastures abandoned in the Depression or during the Second World War. Everybody had tractors, and oldtimers kept Percherons to plow the garden. The land was farmed hard. People kept woodlots because when a new barn was needed, that's where they got the oak to build it. Fencerows were clean. Post-war corn was five dollars per bushel, but you could get more than that for it if you ran it through your cattle. Give a man $100 a month, a house, flour, 25 chickens, 2 hogs, and a cow, and he would bale your hay as long as the sun shone. That was a wrinkle in economic time when the small, diversified eastern farm was stable at last, but—though no one knew it—on the edge of final collapse.

The land was carefully tended, but if you wanted to know something about beavers or deer or turkeys or pileated woodpeckers, you consulted history books and read about the extirpation of these mythical creatures by brave pioneers. "Game" consisted of rabbits and squirrels. The wildlife of the South had been shot out of existence by generations of men who were most comfortable aiming a rifle at something—out of necessity in war or out of craving for protein during depressions. Any pileated woodpeckers sighted were likely to be tacked to the side of a wagon between rabbits, Saturdays in Leesburg. The last beaver had been trapped out of the eastern U.S. before 1900.

One could, and did, spend a youth in northern Virginia after World War II and never see a deer. There were groundhogs in the close-cropped pastures, but no deer. Smothered in the love of a compulsive

River otter, Everglades National Park, Florida. ❧ 21
LUTRA CANADENSIS

Calvinism, the land was well kept, but largely dead.

Is it ironic that today, when the land is not loved, but passed over by interstate highways too rude even to follow its contours, that the deer have returned? Fields quit in the Depression now hear the pileated's rough laugh. They're not fields any more. A few beavers from Michigan were released in Pennsylvania in the fifties, then transplanted to Virginia, from which they repopulated the Southeast. In 1980, it was a discovery to find a beaver-gnawed alder by a Piedmont stream. As the decade closes, beavers occupy every Piedmont stream clean enough to sustain higher life forms. Ospreys nest in Charleston. Turkeys trot the outskirts of Richmond. Beside canoeists, otters ride the Chattahoochee through Atlanta. Mink stalk muskrats in a thousand farm ponds.

By default, we reforested the land in the thirties. We quit shooting everything that moved in the forties. We stopped douching the land with killer poisons in the sixties. In the 1980s, wildlife has returned in an abundance we could only dream of as

22 ❧ *Falls, Great Smoky Mountains*
National Park, Tennessee.

toters of BB guns, setters of skunk deadfalls. The wildlife has returned, the gene pool is clear and deep, enriched and poised to recolonize.

Returning, life seeks flowing water. Once established, it clusters there. Moving water picks up oxygen as it tumbles and detritus as it washes off the land. That feeds crustaceans and fish, and they draw kingfishers and otters. Naiads, newts, wood ducks, and muskrats come to the water, and mink to the muskrats. Floods bring silts that become fertile alluvial soils for buttonbush, box elder, black willow (home to yellow warblers), and river birch (home to downy woodpeckers, which bring prothonotary warblers). A network of systems and dependencies builds skyward to the sycamores and overcup oaks and shagbark hickories that grow in the alluvia.

Alluvial soils are altogether different from those on slopes a few yards away. The soils on the slopes form in place through chemical action gnawing at the underlying rock, then mixing with life at the surface. Such soils are called residual. When they are washed away, gathered into rivulets, streams, creeks, and rivers and deposited by receding floods, they become alluvial—rich mixtures averaging the pH and mineral profiles of the lands in the watershed. They form the bottomlands so prized by early farmers. Today, when the searing summers of the Greenhouse Age wither corn on the slopes, bottomland corn often survives.

Laced with nutrients leached upstream, silky-textured and moist, the alluvial soils support the richest life schemes in the southern Piedmont. In parts of the southern Appalachians, the bottomlands are the only lands worth farming at all. Because alluvia differ so radically from residuals on adjacent slopes, it is not surprising that the alluvial plant communities are fundamentally distinct from those on the slopes, where white oak, black oak, and Spanish oak dominate with pignut and mockernut hickories. At the abrupt edge of the alluvia, a different congress of oaks convenes—water oak, swamp white oak, overcup oak, and a bottomland version of the ubiquitous Spanish or southern red oak called swamp

lands. From microbes in the soil to raptors, fauna thrives at the flowing water's endless catered feast. This is the realm of the spring peeper, the prothonotary warbler, and the red-shouldered hawk. Here dwell the barred owl, the pileated woodpecker, and the wood duck, the spotted sandpiper and its warbler mimic, the waterthrush.

If you would see wildness in the South today, go to the bottomlands. Find running water. Hike if you wish, or drive to an old bridge, park, and sit. A kingfisher rattles under the bridge; an Acadian flycatcher hiccups; a beaver drops a cinderblock into the water; a spotted sandpiper tickles the ripples with its wingtips; a dozen other streamforest beings beckon. Walk the creek and pause, walk and pause. Soon, a tributary will stop you. If you really want to taste what's wild in the South today, to drop back a thousand years and into a life realm running more or less on its own without a planning board's guiding wisdoms, make your visit by canoe.

A canoe—a really good canoe, not an aluminum

Spanish oak. The hillside mockernut yields to the shagbark hickory. Under the unique alluvial canopies stand subdominant ranks which also differ from their dry-land counterparts: alders instead of dogwoods, ironwood instead of redbud, and cross vine instead of trumpet creeper.

Grazing on the alluvial plants, and on one another, is a community of animals peculiar to the bottom-

one that makes ghastly noises and crimps permanently on impact, but, say, a Mad River Explorer with wooden gunwales and cane seats, a craftsman's blend of flex-and-return wood and a sandwiched fiberglass hull—costs about $1,000. That is a sizeable sum, but compared to the cost of a space ship, cheap transport to another world.

If you live in the South, you live within an hour of a navigable stream like the one described above. There, a canoe will float you on a journey deep into time and space, which, on an afternoon's outing, might cover ten miles. In Charlotte, try the Uwharrie. Near Charlottesville, take the Ni or the Po or the North Anna. From Columbia, see the Congaree Swamp from the Congaree River. In Atlanta, the otters on the Chattahoochee *inside* the beltway are waiting to snort at you. From Tampa, try the Peace, the Myakka, or the Withlacoochee. But don't go in April. The red-shouldered hawks might snatch your hat as you pass under a nest. And at any cost, don't get caught on the Withlacoochee at sunset

because the barred owls howl from the nether world and you'll be days calming your cervical lanugo. Limpkins are the banshees of broad daylight on Florida's rivers.

We can be even more specific. If you live in the Raleigh-Durham-Chapel Hill area, get on U.S. 15-501 and go south to the crossing of the Haw River, where an old dam there holds a head of water to power a still-cranking, 19th-century textile mill. Drive another car upstream to the "Chicken Bridge" which carries County Road 1539 across the Haw.

Little wood satyr on smilax, Arkansas. &⟨ 25

EUPTYCHIA CYMELA; SMILAX *SP.*

Slip the canoes into the brown water. The rest of your seven-mile day, you'll glide through the woodlands in the company of hooded mergansers, wood ducks, great blue herons, bald eagles, ospreys, red-shouldered hawks (note the steam engine hiss of the red-tail hawk over nearby slopes), beavers, otters, mink, and muskrats. A brace of wild turkeys may cross ahead of you. The river is gentle on this stretch but will challenge the slightest overconfidence. You can rest and eat and listen on any of a hundred rock ledges sloping to the water. Sights and sounds usurp the senses; water voices laugh and mumble in this new reality. "Egad, what unbelievable refreshment, what fictional adventure! I'm going to spend every free minute here from now on." (You don't, of course, for the river is too special, too intense, and might vanish with familiarity.) Reality narrows to the water's dark silk and to the procession of warblers and mustellids insisting on introduction, inquiring your purpose in their precinct. There comes a time, though, on any river trip—the first or the four hundredth—when the focus slips, unnoticed, inward. The hush and tumble of river life forces an awareness of self in a context old and valid, yet new. There is a spasm in the chest, invulnerable to reason, a jolt of growth in the heart.

The Haw takes a bend, disgorging us into the quiet of the pond upstream from 15-501. Road noise, a mile ahead, intrudes into a canoe-induced awareness.

THE FLOWING WATERS and their bottomlands have always been the most fruitful of the South's life schemes. That became doubly true with the European invasion. The riverine communities defy inspection and exploitation, being in many cases too wet to farm and largely unsuitable for the strip-mining which passes for housing developments in, say, Washington's Northern Virginia suburbs. The good news is that where the waters flow in the South there is wildness.

Today.

Right now!

26 ❧ *(Facing) Great Falls of the Potomac, Virginia.*

You can float any free-flowing river or creek and be virtually guaranteed of a wilderness experience. The crazier the water, in general, the wilder the country it runs through. Take the middle stretch of the Chattooga in northern Georgia, Wilsons Creek in North Carolina, or any of a dozen of the South's other whitewater rollercoasters if the easy-gradient rivers are too tame.

But take them soon. Because the U.S. Army Corps of Engineers has plans for the running water in the South—much of the rest of the country too, but especially the South.

Therein lies an interesting study.

The Great Depression hit most of America like an earthquake, sudden and unexpected. In the South, a region befriended by hard times, it was just another visit by the sweating banker. By then the man behind the mule knew well enough that the federal government was likely to do pretty much as it pleased with him and his land. Resistance had not proved profitable in the past.

In the South, the government elected to combat the Depression by launching a no-quarter assault on the region's rivers. The Depression, it was argued, presented an opportunity to build the nation's infrastructure while providing jobs. In the West, this may have made some economic sense, for damming the Colorado River would at least generate electricity, long-term, and jobs, short-term. In the South, it made no sense at all. There, most rivers follow modest gradients and cut shallowly into the surrounding terrain so that the height differential you get relative to the amount of earth you have to move to get it could not be a cost-effective way to generate electricity. In the South, any power plants associated with dams were to help justify the dams. "Flood control" was the hue and cry.

HYMENOCALLIS OCCIDENTALIS

In the 1930s and 1940s, the Tennessee River and its tributaries were effectively destroyed to build a series of hydroelectric dams. In 1939, 160,000 acres of cypress and tupelo swamp forest were bulldozed into heaps and burned to construct Lake Marion on the Santee and Lake Moultrie on the Cooper River in South Carolina. The lakes store water to cool fossil-fired generators.

After World War II, the full wrath of the Corps and other agencies fell upon the South's rivers. The Piedmont section of the Roanoke River, roughly paralleling the Virginia-North Carolina border, was effectively destroyed with two back-to-back dams drowning 50 miles of bottomlands. One hundred miles or more of the Yadkin-Peedee system vanished under lifeless lakes. An astounding 300 miles of the Catawba—its entire span in the Piedmont and much in the Appalachian province—form a nearly un-broken chain of lakes behind dam after ludicrous dam. Not an inch of the Savannah's 150-mile jour-ney through the Piedmont survived the mid-20th-century hysteria for constructing dams in the South.

Now let's look at Pennsylvania. The Schuylkill skirts Hawk Mountain, then weaves through the Amish farmlands to join the unmolested Delaware at Philadelphia. The magnificent Susquehanna and all its tributaries lace the uplands and the Piedmont, the farthest creek open to eels from the Sargasso Sea and shad from the Atlantic Ocean. Here and there an

Bald cypress swamp, Arkansas.   29

TAXODIUM DISTICHUM

Indian fishing weir funnels the flow in dry times, but the rivers of Pennsylvania are run largely by gravity rather than the U.S. Army. Somehow the people of Pennsylvania take their water from these rivers without detaining them.

There's a famous landscape of the Connecticut River painted by Thomas Cole in the mid-19th century. From the viewer's perspective atop Mt. Holyoke in Massachusetts, the river dreams through Cole's canvas, lapping fields and woodlots. The painting could be duplicated from that vantage today, for the hauntingly beautiful Connecticut still drifts past Holyoke's battlements. The Corps probably knows better than to suggest to the citizens of Massachusetts that they should exchange the Connecticut and its valley for a series of recreational lakes suitable for water skiing three months each year.

This argument has been persuasive, however, in the South. Astoundingly, it still is. As late as the early 1980s, the so-called "Research Triangle" in North Carolina, arguably one of the more socially advanced communities in the region, squandered nearly its entire legacy of free-running water. On the Neuse River upstream of Raleigh, 14,000 acres of narrow bottomlands in a 30-mile stretch were bulldozed and flooded to meet the water "demand" planners anticipate from the growth in the vicinity. The Neuse was a superb stream arcing north of Raleigh and offering what might have been one of the most appealing regional parks in the nation.

The Triangle's supreme environmental achievement, however, occurred 20 miles south of Raleigh on the lower Haw. Until 1980, the Haw contained a four-mile whitewater stretch cascading across a braided bed that changed with every shift in the water level. If it existed today, it would easily be the most important recreational resource in the region. Unfortunately, during the Vietnam War, the Corps exhumed a Depression-era legacy authorizing a dam on the Haw. While attention was elsewhere, the project was funded, and presto—18,000 acres of alluvial (Piedmont, mind you!) hardwood forest was bulldozed, burned, and converted to what the EPA in its environmental impact statement then predicted would be the filthiest body of water in the United States.

And so it appears to be.

Rivers are fed by detritus from the watershed and oxygenated by the tumbling of water over rocks. Rivers support life.

Stop the river behind a dam, and its charge of silt, sewage, and agricultural runoff cooks to algal soup under the summer sun. If the water level were stable, as it tends to be in natural lakes in the glaciated

North, aquatic plants would grow. The lake would then produce its own food supply, and the aquatics would oxygenate the water. But the lakes of the Piedmont, all of which are made by destroying rivers with

Common grackle, Virginia. 🐦 31
QUISCALUS QUISCULA

dams, have wildly fluctuating water lines flooding the edges half the year, exposing sun-baked flats and lifeless clay cuts the rest. No plant community can live in those extremes. The only food comes from the oxygen-gulping algae. The fish which can stand the algal brew are eels, catfish, and carp. Gone are the bass, bream, and grass pickerel of the flowing water.

The Atlantic-bound rivers of the South are dammed all but out of existence. In the North, they are largely intact, or at least free of the high dams drowning the flood plains under vast and lifeless inland seas. Those are the facts. The reasons behind them we must look within ourselves to find.

The major rivers are ruined, but even in the South many of the tributaries are intact. Nearing the sea, feeling the rising tides, the rivers are undammable. Here is wildness.

Just down the coast from Charleston, three rivers merge and braid across an ancient flood plain. The Ashepoo, the Combahee, and the Edisto form and share a joint delta and tidal marsh system perhaps unmatched on the continent in richness and diversity. The wood stork, effectively extinct as a breeding bird in southern Florida, recently has begun to breed in the ACE Basin, raising hopes that here it may persist for a time in North America. The ACE Basin's marshes were once rice fields, cleared of cypress two centuries ago, then diked and graded by forced labor. The old dikes have been breached by storms, and the brackish waters come and go now at the bidding of the moon, lacing and crossing the river's seaward seep. Cypress and tupelo edge in to reassert their patent. A pair of bald eagles warms to a winter sunrise in a moss-draped maple. The aspect is unmistakably southern, undeniably wild.   —*Michael Godfrey*

32 ❧ *Trout stream, Ozark Mountains, Missouri.*
(Facing) Bald eagles, South Carolina.

HALIAEETUS LEUCOCEPHALUS

34 ❧   *Stream, Great Smoky Mountains, Tennessee. More than 600 miles of clear,*
     spring-fed streams flow through the Great Smoky Mountains of Tennessee
     and North Carolina.

Ferns, Great Smoky Mountains, Tennessee. The rain-soaked Smoky ❧ 35
Mountains support a remarkable diversity of plants; 62 species of ferns
have been identified within the national park.

36 ❧ *Ruby-throated hummingbird, Virginia. The only species that breeds east of the Mississippi River, the ruby-throated hummingbird lays eggs the size of peas in a nest made of plant material and spider silk.* ARCHILOCHUS COLUBRIS

American painted lady on red clover, Virginia. Though it bears close resemblance
to a similar species, the American painted lady can be identified by the two large
eyespots on its hind wings. VANESSA VIRGINIENSIS; TRIFOLIUM PRATENSE

38 ❧ *Trout lily, Missouri. One of the first spring ephemerals to bloom, the trout lily is named for its mottled leaves or, as folklore has it, because it appears when trout begin to bite.* ERYTHRONIUM ROSTRATUM

Eastern meadowlark, Loxahatchee National Wildlife Refuge, Florida. ❧ 39
The eastern meadowlark makes its way on foot through grassy fields,
seeking beetles, crickets, and grasshoppers. STURNELLA MAGNA

40 ❧ *Amanita mushroom, Virginia. Only experts can safely distinguish the deadly from the delectable within the genus* Amanita. AMANITA SP. *(Facing) Scott's Run, Virginia. Life abounds in streams and along their edges: a closer look could reveal mayflies, caddis flies, salamanders, toads, and crayfish. In time, thirst brings raccoons, opossums, and squirrels to drink.*

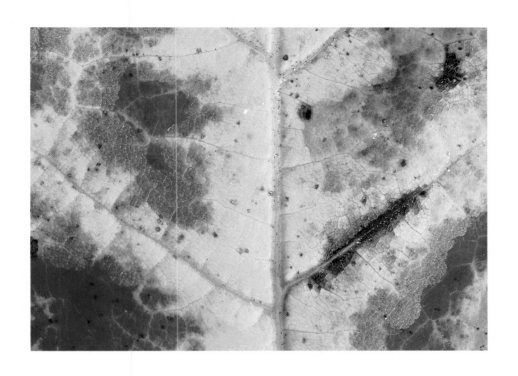

(Facing and above) Sugar maples, Tennessee and West Virginia. ❧ 43
Often associated with New England, the sugar maple also grows in Piedmont
bottomlands and Southern mountains. The shade- and weather-tolerant
tree produces sap that boils down to make syrup. ACER SACCHARUM

44 ❧   *Copperhead, Oklahoma. The copperhead is a pit viper; two pits in front of its eyes contain*
heat sensors that help locate prey. The snake's bite, injecting venom that damages blood vessels
and body tissues, can be fatal to humans. AGKISTRODON CONTORTRIX

American beech, North Carolina. A shade tree found in well-drained lowlands and 🌿 45
rich upland soils, the beech keeps many of its pale copper leaves well into winter.

FAGUS GRANDIFOLIA

Mourning doves, Virginia. Mourning doves puff up their feathers to insulate themselves ❧ 47
from winter's cold. ZENAIDA MACROURA *(Facing) Lowland forest, Virginia.*
Wet, heavy snow clears out branches too weak or brittle to spring back during a thaw.

Sweet gum, South Carolina. Star-shaped leaves and aromatic twigs distinguish the ❧ 49
sweet gum, a pioneer in logged areas and old fields. LIQUIDAMBAR STYRACIFLUA
(Facing) American mountain ash, Dolly Sods, West Virginia. The mountain ash's berries
provide food for birds including ruffed grouse and cedar waxwings. SORBUS AMERICANA

50 ❧ *Red chanterelle, Virginia. Cinnamon-colored chanterelles*
grow under hardwoods in late summer and early fall.
CANTHARELLUS CINNABARINUS

Boletes, Virginia. Most fungi obtain food in one of three ways. Some, like these 🐾 51
bolete mushrooms, grow symbiotically with trees; others feed parasitically on
plants; and still others live on fallen timber, leaves, and other dead matter.

BOLETUS RETIPES

52 🦋 *American copper on oxeye daisy, Virginia. From May to midsummer, coppers are highly visible, feeding on wildflowers in fields and along roadsides.* LYCAENA PHLAEAS AMERICANA; CHRYSANTHEMUM LEUCANTHEMUM   *(Facing) Meadow, Virginia. Between mowings, grass provides food and cover for a community of insects, reptiles, mammals, and birds.*

54 🦋 *Tickseed sunflowers and buckeye butterfly, Maryland. Dense colonies of tickseed sunflowers invade marshes and meadows, ditches and open lowlands.* BIDENS *SP.*; PRECIS COENIA
(Facing) Dickcissel, Roth Prairie Natural Area, Arkansas. A male claims territory with a dry, insistent call that gives him his name: **dick, dick, dick-cissel.** SPIZA AMERICANA

(Facing and above) Green-backed heron and sabal palm, Merritt Island National ❧ 57
Wildlife Refuge, Florida. Merritt Island's salt marshes, swamps, and freshwater
impoundments provide diverse habitats for a wide range of wildlife species.

BUTORIDES STRIATUS; SABAL PALMETTO

58 🌿 *Sabal palms, Florida. Florida's state tree, capped with a crown of shiny spiked leaves, can grow to*
a height of more than 60 feet. SABAL PALMETTO *(Facing) Great egret, Merritt Island, Florida.*
Like other herons, the great egret usually hunts alone. Distinguished from the snowy egret by its
black feet and yellow bill, the bird stalks prey in wetland open areas. CASMERODIUS ALBUS

Snowy egret, Florida. At home in fresh and saltwater marshes, the snowy egret sometimes swoops along 61 *the water's surface, dragging its feet to stir up fish and catching them in its bill.* EGRETTA THULA *(Facing) Merritt Island, Florida. Water moves slowly through marshes, carrying microscopic organisms, fish, and crustaceans that attract large flocks of waterfowl and shorebirds.*

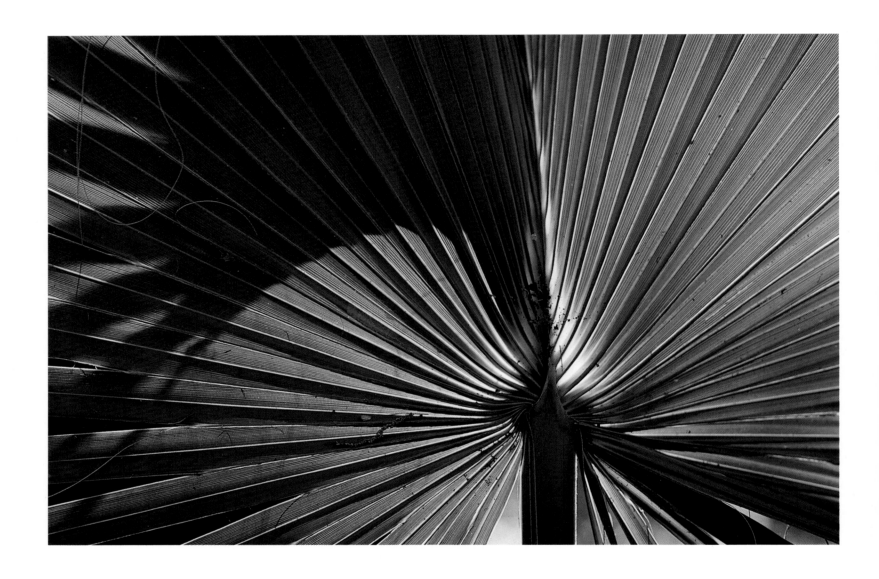

62 🌿 *Saw palmetto, Florida. Spiked, fan-shaped leaves and stalks with stiff spines identify the saw palmetto, a hardy plant that tolerates a wide range of growing conditions.* SERENOA REPENS *(Facing) Green anole on saw palmetto, Florida. Often seen sunning in trees, the anole varies its color to conceal itself from predators, changing from the green of leaves to the brown of bark and stems.* ANOLIS C. CAROLINENSIS; SERENOA REPENS

64 ❧ *American green tree frog on saw palmetto, Florida. The green tree frog inhabits wetland areas, resting by day on leaves.* HYLA CINEREA *(Facing) Corkscrew Swamp Sanctuary, Florida. In both swamps and forests, dead trees provide a feast for insects and birds, and in their hollows creatures as diverse as screech owls, opossums, and raccoons find shelter.*

Golden club, Okefenokee National Wildlife Refuge, Georgia. An aquatic plant of bogs, swamps, and shallow ❧ 67
streams, the golden club has a spike covered with tiny, densely packed flowers. ORONTIUM AQUATICUM
(Facing) Okefenokee Swamp, Georgia. In Okefenokee Swamp, islands, or hammocks, of cypress, pine, and
other trees, edged with sedges and grasses, provide rich habitat for wildlife.

68 ❧ *Alligator and water lettuce, Corkscrew Swamp, Florida. Young alligators usually*
stay close to their mothers for the first year, living on insects, frogs, and crustaceans.
ALLIGATOR MISSISSIPPIENSIS; PISTIA STRATIOTES

Alligator, Wakulla River, Florida. Its range limited by winter temperatures, the alligator can be found in freshwater swamps and marshes as far west as Louisiana and as far north as North Carolina. The reptile digs an underwater burrow for shelter during the coldest months.

ALLIGATOR MISSISSIPPIENSIS

70 ❧ *Crab spider on Queen Anne's lace, Virginia. When an unwary insect comes into range,
the crab spider pounces, seizing its prey with two pairs of powerful front legs. Drawing the
victim near, the spider bites it and injects a deadly poison.* THOMISIDAE; DAUCUS SP.

Flowering dogwood, Virginia. Virginia's state tree brightens woodlands in early
spring; in autumn, its shiny red berries attract robins, blue jays, and cardinals.

CORNUS FLORIDA

72

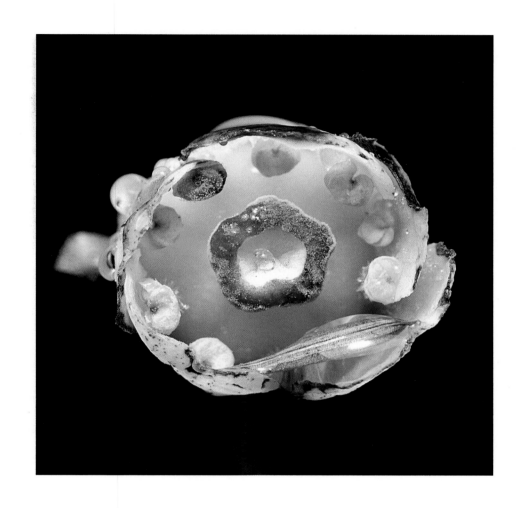

(Above and facing) Indian pipes, Virginia. Indian pipes feed on decaying ❧ 73
matter in forest soils with the help of a fungus associated with their roots.

MONOTROPA UNIFLORA

74 ❧ *Barn owl, Kentucky. The barn owl roosts in tree hollows and empty buildings and hunts*
rodents in open country. Like other owls, it drops soundlessly on its prey; saw-toothed leading
edges on its flight feathers muffle the sound of air against its wings. TYTO ALBA

Cardinal, Virginia. Cardinals carry about three days of fat
reserves, enough to sustain them through most winter storms.

CARDINALIS CARDINALIS

76   *Spring beauty, Oklahoma. Like other wildflower ephemerals, spring beauties emerge during the few weeks between winter's last hard frost and the closing of the leafy canopy.*
CLAYTONIA VIRGINICA

Hickory leaf on algae-covered bracket fungus, Virginia. Bracket fungi decompose the ❧ 77
sapwood of logs and stumps and the heartwood of standing trees. Spores of the fungi
usually enter the tree through a wound in the bark.

Sweet-scented clitocybe, Virginia. This edible, anise-scented mushroom decomposes leaf litter under hardwoods and conifers. CLITOCYBE ODORA *(Facing) Turkey tail fungus (on far side of log), Kentucky. A familiar sight to hikers in eastern forests, turkey tails often grow on fallen oaks.* TRAMETES VERSICOLOR

80 ❧ *Wild azalea, Arkansas. In spring, the pink, trumpet-shaped flowers of wild azalea, also called pinxter, brighten slopes, swamp forests, and rocky summits.* RHODODENDRON NUDIFLORUM *(Facing) Redbud and waterfall, Oklahoma. Oklahoma's state tree flowers in March. According to legend, Judas Iscariot hung himself on a similar tree whose white blossoms turned red with blood or shame.* CERCIS CANADENSIS

Wildflowers in breeze, Natchez Trace Parkway, Mississippi. ❧ 83
(Facing) Bracken fern, Mississippi. Bracken takes hold in dry, sandy,
forest soils and colonizes burned-over areas. PTERIDIUM AQUILANUM

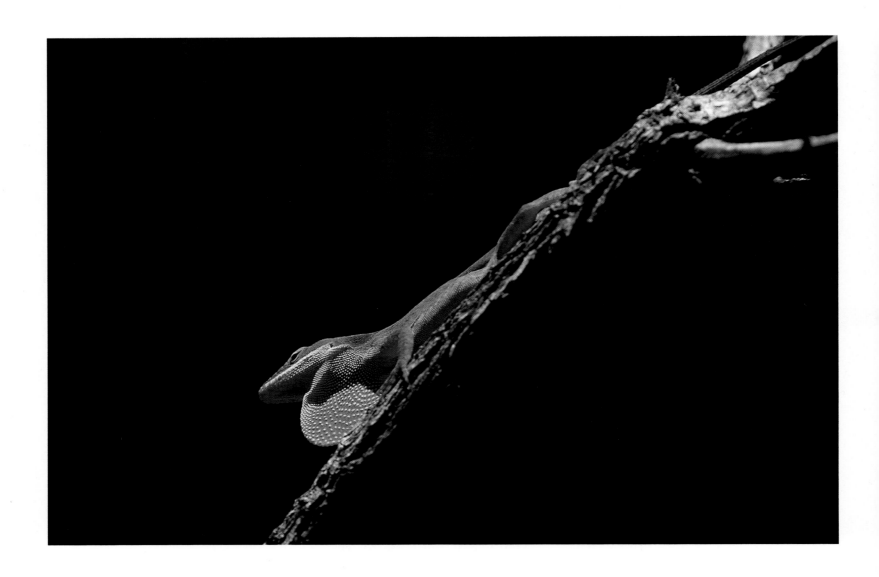

84 ❧ *Green anole, Mississippi. A male anole extends his throat fan to proclaim his territory or lure a mate, sometimes adding to his display with a series of pushups and head bobs.* ANOLIS C. CAROLINENSIS

Hover fly on sensitive briar, Roth Prairie, Arkansas. Hover flies resemble bees   85

and wasps in their markings and flight. Adults feed on nectar; larvae consume as

many as 50 aphids a day. TOXOMERUS SP.; SCHRANKIA UNCINATA

(Above and facing) Northern dusky salamander, Ouachita Mountains, Arkansas. Never straying too far from water, the northern dusky salamander works its way along stream edges looking for insects and their larvae.

DESMOGNATHUS F. FUSCUS

88 ❧ *Gray bats, Tennessee. Only a few caves in North America offer gray bats the right conditions for hibernation. Careless human disturbance of such roosting spots has probably been the cause of a rapid decline in the species.* MYOTIS GRISESCENS

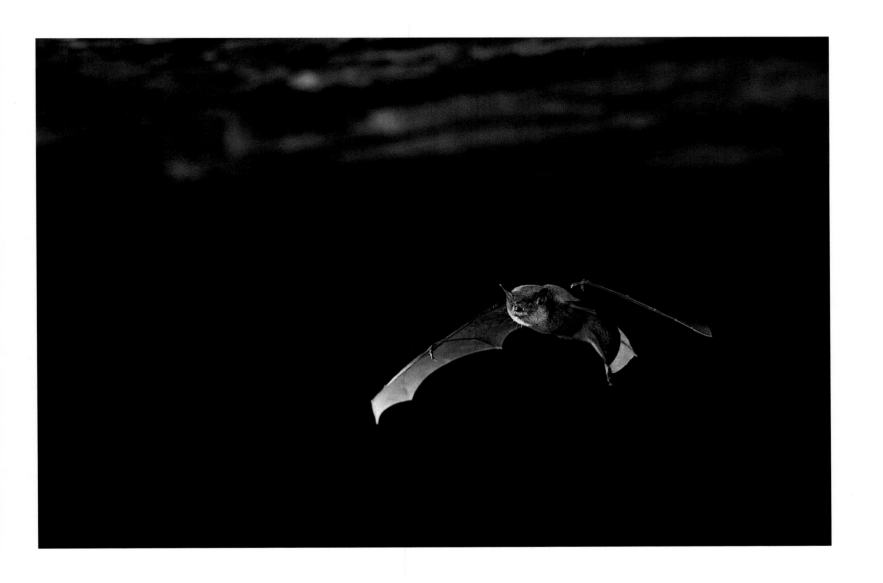

Gray bat, Tennessee. To locate its prey, a gray bat opens its mouth and emits   89
high-frequency sounds. As the sounds rebound from surrounding objects, the bat picks
them up with ears so sensitive that it can pinpoint a mosquito in total darkness.

MYOTIS GRISESCENS

90 ❧ *Southern flying squirrel, Virginia. A fold of skin between front and hind legs enables these nocturnal squirrels to leap and glide as far as 80 yards from one tree to the next in search of acorns and hickory nuts.* GLAUCOMYS VOLANS

Loblolly pines, Assateague Island, Virginia. On Assateague, loblolly pines are ∾ 91
near the northern limit of their range. The fast-growing trees thrive in warmer
climates farther south, where they are an important source of lumber and pulp.

PINUS TAEDA

Great horned owl, Virginia. This powerful predator, named for its ear tufts, preys upon a variety of
creatures from meadow voles to domestic cats. BUBO VIRGINIANUS *(Facing) Woodland aster and black*
locust leaves, Great Smoky Mountains, Tennessee. Fertile soils and ample rainfall support more than
1,500 species of flowering plants in this Appalachian range. ASTER SP.; ROBINIA PSEUDOACACIA

94 ❧ *Baton Rouge lichen, Loxahatchee National Wildlife Refuge, Florida. Baton Rouge lichen colonizes trees, reproducing itself by releasing surface buds that are carried away by wind and water.* CHIODECTON SANGUINEUM

American beech, Virginia. Unlike most trees, beeches retain their ❧ 95

smooth bark through maturity. FAGUS GRANDIFOLIA

Woodchuck, Virginia. Woodchucks inhabit clearings and forest edges and are often seen trundling along ❧ 97
roadsides. They fatten on grass for hibernation, which usually lasts from October through February.
MARMOTA MONAX *(Facing) Scott's Run, Virginia. Most Piedmont forests, such as this one in northern*
Virginia, are dominated by oaks and hickories.

Silver maple and red spruce, Dolly Sods, West Virginia. At the turn of the century, heavy logging and periodic ❧ 99
*fires cleared a climax red spruce forest from these highlands, giving silver maples and other hardwoods a chance
to take hold.* ACER SACCHARINUM; PICEA RUBENS *(Facing) Great Smoky Mountains, North Carolina.
More species of trees grow in the Smokies than in all of Europe.*

100 ⚘ *Fowler's toads, Virginia. A male Fowler's toad clings to his mate's back,*
poised to fertilize her eggs as soon as she deposits them in a nearby puddle.
BUFO WOODHOUSEI FOWLERI

Mockernut hickory leaf, Great Smoky Mountains, Tennessee. Under leaf litter
on the forest floor, bacteria, protozoans, microscopic fungi, and countless other
decomposers recycle nutrients back into the soil.

102 ❧   *Lichens, Arkansas. Where lichens flourish, the air is relatively free of manmade*
pollutants, particularly sulfur dioxide and toxic metals. Sensitivity to these
contaminants makes lichens useful monitors of air quality.

British soldiers lichen, West Virginia. Found only in eastern North America, ❧ 103
British soldiers grow on rocks and decaying wood, and in the sandy soils of
abandoned fields. CLADONIA CRISTATELLA

Crown-tipped coral mushrooms, Virginia. Fallen wood provides a rich medium for crown-tipped coral mushrooms,
named for their resemblance to underwater coral. CLAVICORONA PYXIDATA *(Facing) Boletes, Virginia.*
Bolete mushrooms form tiny sheaths on oak rootlets, obtaining carbon and moisture from the tree. The sheaths
send miles of threadlike cells into the soil that help channel nutrients to the oak. BOLETUS SP.

106 ❧ *Lark sparrows, Texas. Lark sparrows feed in flocks even during mating season. Their song is a varied series of liquid trills sung on the wing as well as on perches or the ground.* CHONDESTES GRAMMACUS

American painted lady on verbena, Alabama. The painted lady
recognizes its favorite flowers with taste organs on its legs.
VANESSA VIRGINIENSIS; VERBENA *SP.*

108 ❧ *Summer grapes, Virginia. Raccoons, opossums, and more than 100 species*
of birds feed on wild grapes, dispersing the seeds in their travels.
VITIS AESTIVALIS

Catbrier, South Carolina. The catbrier wraps its tendrils around trees and   ❧ 109
shrubs, growing in dense, thorny tangles that can climb to over ten feet.

SMILAX BONANOX

Blue dasher on arrowhead, Virginia. Like other dragonflies, the blue dasher has two pairs of wings that move with *remarkable coordination, enabling the insect to hover, fly forward, or fly backward.* PACHYDIPLAX LONGIPENNIS; SAGITTARIA LATIFOLIA *(Facing) Arrowhead, Virginia. A plant of stream edges, marshes, and swamps, the arrowhead produces potato-like tubers harvested by muskrats and dabbling ducks.* SAGITTARIA LATIFOLIA

112 🪶 *Green-backed heron, Everglades National Park, Florida. The green-backed heron can extend its neck the length of its torso to pluck fish from the water.*
BUTORIDES STRIATUS

Tupelo swamp, Mississippi. The roots and buttressed lower trunk of the swamp ❧ 113
tupelo can withstand immersion for months during the growing season.

Key deer, Florida. Key deer, a subspecies of the white-tail, stand two feet tall at the shoulder. The endangered deer live only on the Florida Keys, where they browse on palms and mangrove shoots. ODOCOILEUS VIRGINIANUS CLAVIUM

(Facing) Saw palmettos and pines, Florida. Saw palmettos thrive in the dry, sandy soils of southern pine forests. The stems of the fire-resistant plant run along the ground, supporting fans of blade-like leaves. SERENOA REPENS

116 ❧ *Yellow-crowned night heron, "Ding" Darling National Wildlife Refuge, Florida. While building a nest in a mangrove, a male yellow-crowned night heron spreads his feathers in courtship display.* NYCTICORAX VIOLACEUS
(Facing) Little blue heron and mangroves, Florida. One of the most common wading birds in the South, the little blue heron can be seen along the coast from New York to Texas and inland as far as Oklahoma. EGRETTA CAERULEA

118 ❧ *(Above and facing) Anhinga, Florida. With feathers that retain more water than most, anhingas must stretch their wings to dry in the sun. The birds use their serrated bills to preen feathers and spear fish.* ANHINGA ANHINGA

Barrier island, Georgia. Ghostly stands of dead trees, remnants of forests choked   ❧ 121
by shifting dunes and flooded with salt water, are common on the barrier islands
of the Georgia coast. (Facing) Spindrift, Outer Banks, North Carolina.

Sand patterns, Outer Banks, North Carolina. (Facing) Salt marsh, St. Marks 123
National Wildlife Refuge, Florida. Salt marshes rival the most fertile bottomlands
in their ability to capture the sun's energy, recycle it, and support life.

124 🖎 *Sea oats, Outer Banks, North Carolina. South of the Chesapeake Bay, sea oats are the dominant grass along coastal beaches. The plant slows eroding winds at ground level, and long tap roots help stabilize front-line dunes.* UNIOLA PANICULATA *(Facing) Willet, Virginia. Willets probe the shore for fish, fiddler crabs, and mollusks.* CATOPTROPHORUS SEMIPALMATUS

126 🐾 *Dowitchers, Merritt Island, Florida. Gathering in flocks for protection, dowitchers extract larvae, worms, and snails from mudflats.*

LIMNODROMUS *SP.*

Canada geese, Chincoteague National Wildlife Refuge, Virginia. In the 1960s, a female Canada 🪶 127
goose with a broken wing wintered here with her mate. Since then, the resident population,
drawn by freshwater impoundments and aquatic vegetation, has grown to 250. During
migration, the number swells to 2,000. BRANTA CANADENSIS

128 ❧ *Red-winged blackbird, Okefenokee Swamp, Georgia. Male red-wings have their breeding plumage by their second year. The polygamous birds flash red epaulets edged in yellow to defend their territory and attract mates.*
AGELAIUS PHOENICEUS

Red-winged blackbirds, Maryland. Following breeding season, red-wings sometimes ❧ 129
flock by the thousands with cowbirds, grackles, starlings, and rusty blackbirds.

AGELAIUS PHOENICEUS

130 ❧ *Cattails, South Carolina. Dense stands of cattails grow along edges of ponds and freshwater marshes. In autumn, the stalks and leaves die back, and the flower cylinders release thousands of seeds to the wind.* TYPHA *SP.*

Young red spruce, Gaudineer Scenic Area, Monongahela National Forest, West Virginia. 🦋 131
A 50-acre remnant of the spruce forest that once covered the West Virginia highlands,
Gaudineer includes some 300-year-old red spruces as well as second growth.

PICEA RUBENS

132 ❧ *Black bear cub, Great Smoky Mountains, Tennessee. Though mainly nocturnal, black bears also forage during the day for berries, roots, and insects. A cub is never far from its mother, who can charge at 30 mph to defend her young.* URSUS AMERICANUS *(Facing) Daisy fleabane, Great Smoky Mountains, Tennessee. Early settlers in America kept fleabane in their houses to repel fleas and other insect pests.* ERIGERON SP.

Black swallowtail, Arkansas. At night, butterflies hang upside down with their wings folded, securing themselves ❧ 135
to leaves or twigs with little hooks on their feet. After daybreak, they flatten their wings in the sun to warm up
for flight. PAPILIO POLYXENES ASTERIUS *(Facing) Tiger swallowtail on blackberry blossoms, West Virginia.*
The 27 North American species of swallowtail live mainly in the South. PAPILIO GLAUCUS

Buckeye, Virginia. Brilliant eyespots on the buckeye's wings may startle would-be predators, 137
giving the butterfly a chance to dart away. PRECIS COENIA *(Facing) Buttercups,*
Monongahela National Forest, West Virginia. More than 20 buttercup species bloom in
fields and roadsides in the Southeast from April to June. RANUNCULUS *SP.*

138 🐾 *Eastern box turtle, Virginia. A hinge on its lower shell enables the eastern box turtle to close up tightly when danger threatens.* TERRAPENE C. CAROLINA *(Facing) Sugar maple and stream, Great Smoky Mountains, Tennessee. In late summer, trees grow a cell layer between the twigs and leaf stems, closing off the flow of water and minerals to the leaves. Deprived of chlorophyl, a sugar maple reveals its gold.* ACER SACCHARUM

140 🦋 *Ring-billed gulls, Outer Banks, North Carolina. The South's most common gull is mainly a scavenger,*
combing beaches for fish and garbage. LARUS DELAWARENSIS *(Facing) American beachgrass, Maryland.*
American beachgrass pioneers dunes with fast-growing rootstocks that anchor shifting sands. The plant is also
called "compass grass" for the arcs its blades trace in the sand on windy days. AMMOPHILA BREVILIGULATA

141

142 ❦ *Wood stork and sabal palms, Florida. The largest nesting colonies of wood storks are in Florida, where their numbers have dwindled by 90 percent in the past 30 years. Droughts and human manipulations of the water table will probably eliminate the species.*
MYCTERIA AMERICANA; SABAL PALMETTO

Lesser snow geese, Maryland. Lesser snow geese follow traditional routes from their nesting grounds *in the Arctic to winter habitat along the Gulf and Atlantic coasts. Through the ages, they have adapted as natural forces altered the landscape, but humankind's more rapid and destructive changes severely test these waterfowl and every other wild species.* CHEN C. CAERULESCENS

I appreciate all the help from friends in the U.S. Fish and Wildlife Service, state parks, and The Nature Conservancy. I am particularly indebted to Dr. Jerome Jackson of Mississippi State University and Freeman Thomas of Jacksonville, Arkansas, who have been teachers as well as friends.

Bates Littlehales

I am especially grateful to Dr. Thomas O. Perry, former professor of forestry at North Carolina State University, former fellow board member of the North Carolina Nature Conservancy, and lifelong student of land use in the South. Over the years, Tom has noted our predecessors' imprints on the land. His unpublished paper, "The Role of Man in the Wilderness," puts forth the view that European man holds no first patent here on large-scale agriculture. My deepest debt is to Herman F. Ambers, who made the woods and fields of my Northern Virginia childhood glow with wonder. I hope that I might someday give as lavish a gift.

Michael Godfrey

Places to Visit

Before you visit a state or federally owned natural area, call or write for the most recent information on weather, facilities, fees, and hours. There are no guarantees that you will see certain species, but your chances are greatly improved if you go when conditions are favorable.

ALABAMA

William B. Bankhead National Forest

P.O. Box 278
Double Springs, Alabama 35553
telephone: (205) 489-5111

Located in northwestern Alabama, Bankhead National Forest encompasses waterfalls, bluffs, canyons, and scattered stands of old-growth hardwood. Within the borders of the national forest, the Sipsey Wilderness offers hiking trails, camping, and canoeing along a 30-mile stretch of the Sipsey River. *Best times to visit: summer and fall.*

Dauphin Island Sanctuary

c/o Dauphin Island Park and Beach Board
P.O. Box 97
Dauphin Island, Alabama 36528
telephone: (205) 861-3607

Dauphin Island, a 14-mile-long barrier strip off the coast of Alabama, is leased to the Audubon Society by the state. Migrating songbirds pass through the sanctuary in spring and fall, and shorebirds comb the tidal flats for food year-round. *Best times to visit: spring and fall.*

Wheeler National Wildlife Refuge

Route 4
Box 250
Decatur, Alabama 35603
telephone: (205) 351-0248

Located in northern Alabama in the Tennessee River Valley, Wheeler National Wildlife Refuge is an important wintering area for waterfowl. Snow geese begin arriving between October 15 and November 15, and the greatest number of waterfowl gather in December and January. Waterbirds are numerous through fall and winter. When the water level of Wheeler Lake, a manmade reservoir created by the TVA, is low in late August, shorebirds can be seen on the mudflats. *Best time to visit: winter.*

ARKANSAS

Ouachita National Forest

P.O. Box 1270
Hot Springs, Arkansas 71902
telephone: (501) 321-5202

Covering 1.6 million acres in west-central Arkansas and southeastern Oklahoma, Ouachita National Forest includes campgrounds, scenic drives, five wilderness areas, 350 miles of hiking trails, and float trips along a 35-mile stretch of the Ouachita River. *Best time to visit: year-round.*

Ozark National Forest

P.O. Box 1008
Russellville, Arkansas 72801
telephone: (501) 968-2354

The Ozark National Forest includes more than one million acres stretching from north-central Arkansas south to the Ouachita Mountains. Over 500 species of trees and woody plants grow here; oak and hickory are the dominant hardwoods. The 161-mile-long Ozark Highlands hiking trail crosses the forest, with campsites along the way. Buffalo River, Big Piney Creek, and several other streams are suitable for canoeing. *Best times to visit: spring and fall.*

St. Francis National Forest

P.O. Box 1008
Russellville, Arkansas 72801
telephone: (501) 968-2354

The St. Francis National Forest is located in east-central Arkansas along the Mississippi River. Much of the forest is on Crowley's Ridge, some 200 feet above the river. White oak, red oak, and black hickory predominate on the ridge, while beech and tulip poplar cover lower slopes. The ridge supports flora distinctly different from that found in the flatter parts of Arkansas and Missouri. *Best times to visit: spring and fall.*

FLORIDA

Blowing Rocks Preserve

The Nature Conservancy
1353 Palmetto Avenue
Winter Park, Florida 32789
telephone: (407) 628-5887

Located on Jupiter Island in southeastern Florida, Blowing Rocks Preserve features limestone outcroppings carved by the constant pounding of the Atlantic Ocean. Waves surge through blow holes in the rock, creating plumes of water visible for miles. Beach creeper and beach star, both rare in Florida, are found on the 113-acre preserve, as well as the more common red mangrove. Endangered green, leatherback, and loggerhead turtles come ashore at night from May until August to bury their eggs on the beach. *Contact The Nature Conservancy for more information and best time to visit.*

Corkscrew Swamp Sanctuary

Route 6
Box 1875-A
Naples, Florida 33964
telephone: (813) 657-3771

Corkscrew Swamp lies within the Big Cypress Swamp in southwestern Florida. Administered by the National Audubon Society, Corkscrew contains Florida's last remaining stand of virgin bald cypresses (some more than 500 years old) and one of the last remaining colonies of wood storks in the United States. In spring and summer, swallow-tailed kites soar above the swamp; in winter, a variety of warblers comes through. Wading birds and alligators can be seen here year-round. A 1.75-mile-long boardwalk winds through the preserve's major habitats: wetland prairie, pond cypress swamp, woods of slash pine and saw palmetto, and immense bald cypresses towering over lush undergrowth. *Best times to visit: fall and winter. Entrance fee.*

Merritt Island National Wildlife Refuge

P.O. Box 6504
Titusville, Florida 32782
telephone: (407) 867-0667

The refuge covers part of Canaveral Peninsula and Merritt Island and borders the Kennedy Space Flight Center. Salt marshes, impoundments, and mangrove swamps provide feeding grounds and nesting habitat for waterfowl, songbirds, shorebirds, raptors, waders, and waterbirds; in all, more than 310 species of birds have been sighted. More threatened and endangered species live here than in any other refuge in the United States. *Best times to visit: fall, winter, and spring.*

Everglades National Park

P.O. Box 279
Homestead, Florida 33030
telephone: (305) 247-6211

During the wet season, a river six inches deep and 50 miles wide flows through the sawgrass of the Everglades and empties into Florida Bay. The marshland supports an amazing variety of shore-birds, water birds, waders, and waterfowl year-round. The best time to see them is in winter, when lower water levels cause wildlife to concentrate at pools. The park is home to alligators and the more rare and reclusive crocodile, which inhabits salt-water estuaries at the tip of Florida. The park offers a motel, campgrounds, canoeing, board-walk trails, and marked drives through wildlife areas. *Best time to visit: winter. Entrance fee.*

J. N. "Ding" Darling National Wildlife Refuge

1 Wildlife Drive
Sanibel, Florida 33957
telephone: (813) 472-1100

This 5,014-acre refuge on San-ibel Island encompasses both fresh and saltwater wetlands. Migrating songbirds come through in spring and fall. Winter brings a variety of waterfowl and large numbers of shore-birds, including black-bellied plovers, ruddy turnstones, and sanderlings. In summer, Wilson's plovers, Sandwich terns, and least terns frequent nearby coastal beaches. Alligators, roseate spoonbills, ospreys, and moor-hens stay year-round. About 300 species of birds, 30 species of mammals, and 50 kinds of rep-tiles and amphibians have been identified. Along the five-mile-long scenic drive, a variety of wildlife can be seen. *Best time to visit: spring. Entrance fee.*

St. Marks National Wildlife Refuge

P.O. Box 68
St. Marks, Florida 32355
telephone: (904) 925-6121

St. Marks National Wildlife Refuge stretches along the Apa-lachee Bay in the Gulf of Mexico. The 65,000-acre refuge, an important wintering ground for waterfowl, includes coastal marsh, sand flats, freshwater impoundments, small islands of saw palmetto and slash pine, and 18,000 acres of marsh wilderness. The area is an important win-tering ground for waterfowl. Foot trails and marked drives offer a chance to see shorebirds, wading birds, bald eagles, arma-dillos, river otters, alligators, and elusive bobcats and Florida black bears. *Best times to visit: fall, winter, and spring. Entrance fee.*

GEORGIA

Cumberland Island National Seashore

P.O. Box 806
St. Marys, Georgia 31558
telephone: (912) 882-4337

More than 300 species of birds have been sighted on the south-ernmost and largest of Georgia's Sea Islands. Wading birds occupy the sound side of the bar-rier island, warblers and buntings are found in upland forests, and shorebirds can be seen on the beach. Access to the island is only by boat. Campsites are available by reservation. *Best time to visit: winter.*

Piedmont National Wildlife Refuge

Route 1
Box 670
Round Oak, Georgia 31038
telephone: (912) 986-5441

Piedmont National Wildlife Refuge is located north of Macon and just east of the Ocmulgee River. A forest of loblolly and shortleaf pine and mixed hard-woods covers most of the 35,000-acre refuge, and water impoundments make the refuge a valuable wintering area for waterfowl. Resident bird species include the endangered red-cockaded woodpecker, which makes its home in stands of old-growth pine. Visitors have the best chance of seeing this rare species in May and June, when the woodpeckers are nesting. Spring and fall migrations bring large numbers of birds—about 200 species have been identified at the refuge. Walking trails and an auto route provide oppor-tunities for viewing wildlife. *Best times to visit: spring and fall.*

Okefenokee National Wildlife Refuge

Route 2
Box 338
Folkston, Georgia 31537
telephone: (912) 496-3331

The refuge covers nearly 400,000 acres of the Okefenokee, a vast area of marsh and swamp forest in southeastern Georgia near the Florida border. Several endan-gered species find habitat here, among them the red-cockaded woodpecker, wood stork, bald eagle, and gopher tortoise. The refuge's wetlands attract large numbers of wading birds, including sandhill cranes. Okefenokee National Wildlife Refuge is also one of the best places in the United States to see alligators. The refuge and its wildlife can be seen from boardwalks, canoe trails, hiking trails, and an auto tour; campsites are also available. *Best times to visit: fall, winter, and spring. Entrance fee.*

Savannah National Wildlife Refuge

Box 8487
Savannah, Georgia 31412
telephone: (912) 944-4415

Savannah National Wildlife Refuge is the largest in the Savannah Coastal Refuge system, which stretches 100 miles from Pinkney Island NWR on the southern tip of South Carolina to Wolf Island NWR near Darien, Georgia. Hardwood swamps, freshwater marshes, tidal creeks and rivers, and impoundments cover most of the refuge's 25,000 acres. Wood storks come through in spring and eagles in winter. Ospreys can be seen during most of the year. A driving tour and walking trails give access to some of the refuge's wildlife and their habitats, but more than half the refuge is hardwood swamp and can only be reached by boat. *Best times to visit: summer and winter.*

KENTUCKY

John James Audubon State Park

P.O. Box 576
Henderson, Kentucky 42420
telephone: (502) 826-2247

The 700-acre Audubon State Park is a rolling, wooded area along the Ohio River near Henderson, Kentucky, where John James Audubon observed and drew wildlife. Within the park, a 325-acre nature preserve with 5.5 miles of trails is noted for woodpeckers and for migrating warblers in spring and fall. A wide variety of wildflowers blooms in spring. The park's Audubon Museum displays some of the artist's memorabilia and original artwork. A campground and five primitive cottages are available for overnight stays. *Best times to visit: spring and fall. Entrance fee to the museum.*

Daniel Boone National Forest

100 Vaught Road
Winchester, Kentucky 40391
telephone: (606) 745-3100

Daniel Boone National Forest encompasses a rugged landscape of deep valleys, steep slopes, natural arches, and hundreds of miles of sandstone cliffs in eastern Kentucky. About 1,300 species of trees and plants, including 40 species of orchids, thrive here; oak, hickory, and pine grow on the ridgetops, and eastern hemlock, poplar, and beech in the valleys. Ruffed grouse, warblers, red and gray

foxes, fox squirrels, muskrats, and beaver are common. Scenic drives, hiking trails, and campgrounds offer recreation opportunities. *Best times to visit: fall and spring.*

LOUISIANA

Kisatchie National Forest

2500 Shreveport Highway
Pineville, Louisiana 71360
telephone: (318) 473-7160

Kisatchie National Forest includes seven separate districts, five in central Louisiana and two near Shreveport. The system encompasses swamps and bayous, lakes, and pine uplands. Endangered red-cockaded woodpeckers nest in large longleaf and loblolly pines. The Kisatchie Wilderness, with its bluffs, rock outcrops, and fast-flowing streams, has a landscape very different from most of Louisiana. The Saline Bayou National Scenic River, lined with bald cypresses and bottomland hardwoods, can be explored by canoe. Hiking trails and a scenic drive wind through the national forest. *Best times to visit: spring and fall.*

MARYLAND

Assateague Island National Seashore

Route 611
7206 National Seashore Lane
Berlin, Maryland 21811
telephone: (301) 641-1441

A 37-mile-long barrier island off the coasts of Maryland and Vir-

ginia, Assateague attracts a variety of wading birds, shorebirds, and waterfowl. Most of the Maryland portion of the island is managed by the National Park Service. To the south, on the Virginia portion of the island, Chincoteague National Wildlife Refuge has impoundments which attract even greater numbers of birds. The national seashore offers walking trails, camping, and canoeing. *Best times to visit: spring and fall.*

Blackwater National Wildlife Refuge

2145 Key Wallace Drive
Cambridge, Maryland 21613
telephone: (301) 228-2677

Located near Cambridge on the eastern shore of the Chesapeake Bay, Blackwater National Wildlife Refuge covers approximately 16,700 acres of tidal marsh, open ponds, agricultural fields, and loblolly pine and mixed hardwood forests. The refuge is noted for large populations of waterfowl in spring and fall, especially Canada geese, mallards, and American black ducks. White-tailed deer, bald eagles, and the endangered Delmarva fox squirrel are here, too. A three-mile drive winds through habitats where a range of wildlife is often visible. *Best times to visit: fall and winter.*

MISSISSIPPI

Gulf Islands National Seashore

3500 Park Road
Ocean Springs,
Mississippi 39564
telephone: (601) 875-9057

A 400-acre area of the Mississippi coast in addition to Ship, Horn, and Petit Bois Islands just off the mainland comprise Gulf Islands National Seashore. On the coast, salt marshes provide habitat for clapper rails and screech, barred, and great horned owls. Visitors are likely to see brown pelicans, cormorants, ospreys, and bald eagles. During spring and fall migrations, strong winds sometimes force a variety of warblers, buntings, and other land birds to rest here in large numbers. Shorebirds are present year-round. From March through October, scheduled ferry trips are offered to Ship Island. Access during other months, and to Horn and Petit Bois Islands at any time, must be privately arranged. There is a campground on the mainland. *Best times to visit: spring, summer, and fall.*

Noxubee National Wildlife Refuge

Route 1
Box 142
Brooksville, Mississippi 39739
telephone: (601) 323-5548

Noxubee National Wildlife Refuge in east-central Mississippi covers almost 47,000 acres. Oaks, hickories, and loblolly pines dominate the refuge's extensive upland forests, and in the bottomlands along the Noxubee River, cypresses and other hardwoods grow. In late summer, wading birds feed in the shallows of two manmade lakes. Fall brings thousands of ducks and geese. Year-round residents include Canada geese, alligators, and red-cockaded woodpeckers. The refuge has established short hiking trails and primitive campsites. *Best times to visit: fall and winter.*

MISSOURI

Ozark National Forest
(see Arkansas)

NORTH CAROLINA

Cape Hatteras National Seashore

Route 1
Box 675
Manteo, North Carolina 27954
telephone: (919) 473-2111

Cape Hatteras National Seashore extends for 70 miles along the Outer Banks of North Carolina, across Bodie, Hatteras, and Okracoke Islands. The barrier islands include beaches, sand dunes, marshes, and maritime forests of cedar, yaupon holly, and laurel and live oak. Thousands of snow geese and other waterfowl winter at Pea Island National Wildlife Refuge on Hatteras Island. Shorebirds, raptors, and songbirds can be seen in winter and during fall and spring migrations. Walking trails and campsites afford opportunities to experience the seashore. *Best time to visit: year-round.*

Great Smoky Mountains National Park
(see Tennessee)

Nags Head Woods Preserve

701 West Ocean Acres Drive
Kill Devil Hills,
North Carolina 27948
telephone: (919) 441-2525

Near Kitty Hawk on the Outer Banks of North Carolina, The Nature Conservancy's Nags Head Woods Preserve has dunes, marshes, pine hammocks, and freshwater ponds. The 700-acre preserve contains one of the best remaining examples of mid-Atlantic maritime forest, with typical salt- and wind-tolerant trees and shrubs such as redbay and wax myrtle. Protected by the dunes, inland species such as American beech, hickory, and hop hornbeam grow here as well. The preserve provides habitat for 13 species of birds threatened or endangered in North Carolina. The preserve is only open 15 hours each week to protect the area from overuse. *Best times to visit: spring and fall.*

Green Swamp Preserve

The Nature Conservancy
Carr Mill
Suite 223
Carrboro, North Carolina 27510
telephone: (919) 967-7007

Green Swamp Preserve, nearly 16,000 acres of wetland habitat in southeastern North Carolina, is managed by The Nature Conservancy. The preserve encompasses shrub bog, longleaf pine savannah, white cedar swamp, and loblolly pine forest. At least 14 species of carnivorous plants can be found among the abundant flora. Other inhabitants include alligators, eastern diamondback rattlesnakes, and red-cockaded woodpeckers. Call or write the North Carolina Nature Conservancy in advance if you plan to visit; field trips with guides are available.

OKLAHOMA

Ouachita National Forest
(see Arkansas)

SOUTH CAROLINA

Carolina Sandhills National Wildlife Refuge

Route 2
Box 330
McBee, South Carolina 29101
telephone: (803) 335-8401

Located in northeastern South Carolina, the 46,000-acre refuge is named for the area's deep layer of sandy topsoil. Forests of longleaf pine and pockets of scrub oak cover most of the refuge. Wood ducks and a few Canada geese are year-round residents. More colonies of red-cockaded woodpeckers live here than in all other national wildlife refuges combined. To make it easier to see the birds in spring, white bands mark their nesting trees.

Wildlife can be viewed in several ways: on an auto tour, on walking trails, or from a photographic blind. *Best times to visit: fall, winter, and spring.*

Francis Beidler Forest in Four Holes Swamp

Route 1
Box 600
Harleyville,
South Carolina 29448
telephone: (803) 462-2150

Near Charleston, South Carolina, the National Audubon Society manages a 5,800-acre remnant of swamp forest that contains the largest remaining virgin stand of tupelo gum and bald cypress trees in the world. Many of these are thought to be 1,000 years old. Springs and runoff feed Four Holes Swamp. In the wet seasons, usually winter and spring, the swamp is a shallow, flowing river. In summer and fall, the flow shrinks to a maze of creeks and interconnected pools. From the boardwalk, lizards, turtles, snakes, prothonotary warblers, and songbirds can be seen year-round. *Best time to visit: spring. Entrance fee.*

TENNESSEE

Reelfoot National Wildlife Refuge

4343 Highway 157
Union City, Tennessee 38261
telephone: (901) 538-2481

Stretching from northwestern Tennessee into Kentucky, Reelfoot National Wildlife Refuge is a major stopover and wintering area for waterfowl of the Mississippi Flyway. A swamp forest of towering bald cypresses borders Reelfoot Lake, and vegetation on the lake's surface and emergent grasses provide rich habitat for birds and other wildlife. Bald eagles stay through the winter, and some nest here. In spring, migrating songbirds, shorebirds, and wading birds come through in large numbers. Summer is the best time to look for an unusual variety of turtles, non-poisonous snakes, and salamanders. Other wildlife can be spotted along a boardwalk and a scenic drive. *Best times to visit: fall and winter.*

Great Smoky Mountains National Park

Gatlinburg, Tennessee 37738
telephone: (615) 436-1200

Straddling the Tennessee-North Carolina border, Great Smoky Mountains National Park contains 16 peaks with elevations over 6,000 feet. More than 1,500 species of flowering plants grow in the haze-shrouded mountains, and more mushroom species grow here than anywhere else in the United States. The largest stands of virgin forest in the east are protected within the park. Hardwoods flourish in the lower elevations, while spruce, fir, and hemlock cover slopes and ridges. From April to July, wildflowers and rhododendrons bloom. Black bears are often seen foraging in the early morning and late afternoon. The park offers 900 miles of trails and extensive scenic drives, a range of organized nature walks and evening programs, and a number of campgrounds. *Best time to visit: year-round.*

TEXAS

Aransas National Wildlife Refuge

P.O. Box 100
Austwell, Texas 77950
telephone: (512) 286-3559

Aransas National Wildlife Refuge covers almost 55,000 acres of grasslands and tidal marshes along the southeastern coast of Texas. Its mild climate and abundant food supplies attract more than 350 species of birds. The endangered whooping crane winters here, and spring migration brings warblers. Brown pelicans live in the area year-round, and alligators lurk in inland freshwater ponds. A 16-mile auto tour and 6 miles of walking trails give views of different habitats and chances to see wildlife. *Best times to visit: winter and spring.*

Big Thicket National Preserve

3785 Milam
Beaumont, Texas 77701
telephone: (409) 839-2689

Big Thicket National Preserve in eastern Texas is a biological crossroads where flora and fauna characteristic of many regions co-exist in an 85,000-acre area. There are four major plant associations: pine savannah, flatlands palmetto, mixed hardwood and pine forest, and floodplain forest with cypress sloughs. In such diverse habitats, an abundance of wildlife species thrives. A large variety of wildflowers and four of the five kinds of carnivorous plants found in North America grow here. Hiking trails give access to the varying terrain. *Best times to visit: spring and fall.*

VIRGINIA

Chincoteague National Wildlife Refuge

P.O. Box 62
Chincoteague, Virginia 23336
telephone: (804) 336-6122

Chincoteague National Wildlife Refuge is located on the Virginia end of Assateague Island, a barrier strip with wide, sandy beaches, low dunes, maritime forest, and bayside marshes. The refuge is an important stopover and resting place for birds migrating along the Atlantic Flyway. Water impoundments enhance the natural habitat for wildlife, and thousands of waterfowl winter here. Shorebirds come through during spring and fall migration, and marsh birds are here from mid-spring to late fall. Whitetail and small, oriental sika deer live in the pine forest, and wild ponies graze on marsh grasses. Auto tours and walking trails give access to areas for viewing wildlife. *Best times to visit: fall and spring.*

Great Falls Park

P.O. Box 66
Great Falls, Virginia 22066
telephone: (703) 285-2965

At Great Falls, the Potomac River becomes a torrent as it drops 76 feet over a series of huge boulders. During spring runoff, the flow over the quarter-mile-long falls is especially dramatic. Oaks, beeches, sycamores, pawpaws, and trailing arbutus grow along the banks of the river. Beavers, wood ducks, Canada geese, and bald eagles are among the wildlife. In spring, wildflowers bloom throughout the park. There are more than 12 miles of walking trails with views of Great Falls and 60-foot cliffs along the Potomac River. *Best times to visit: fall, winter, and spring. Entrance fee.*

Back Bay National Wildlife Refuge

P.O. Box 6286
4005 Sandpiper Road
Virginia Beach, Virginia 23456
telephone: (804) 721-2412

Located on the coast of southeastern Virginia, Back Bay National Wildlife Refuge is an important stopover for birds of the Atlantic Flyway. The refuge's beaches, marshes, vegetated dunes, shrublands, inland mudflats, and shallow waters of the bay all provide feeding grounds for birds and other wildlife. The refuge offers habitat for a variety of birds, including snow geese and endangered piping plovers, peregrine falcons, and bald eagles. In spring, songbirds come through; in summer, wading birds and marshbirds are abundant; autumn brings waterfowl, raptors, and shorebirds. More than 13 miles of dikes and hiking trails pass through many of the refuge's habitats. *Best times to visit: fall and winter. Entrance fee.*

Great Dismal Swamp National Wildlife Refuge

3100 Desert Road
P.O. Box 349
Suffolk, Virginia 23434
telephone: (804) 986-3705

Located in southeastern Virginia and northeastern North Carolina, the Great Dismal Swamp contains five different forest types: pine, tupelo-bald cypress, Atlantic white cedar, maple-blackgum, and sweetgum-oak-poplar. Lake Drummond, 3,100 acres in area, six feet deep, its waters blackened by cypress and tupelo, lies in the middle of the refuge and provides a resting place for migrating waterfowl. Dwarf trillium, silky camellia, swamp azalea, and the rare log fern are protected here. Two southern species of birds, Swainson's warbler and Wayne's warbler (a southern subspecies of the black-throated green warbler), are occasionally sighted. Visitors can see the swamp and its wildlife by canoe or from hiking trails. *Best time to visit: spring.*

WEST VIRGINIA

Monongahela National Forest

200 Sycamore Street
Elkins, West Virginia 26241
telephone: (304) 636-1800

The Monongahela National Forest covers more than 900,000 acres in the rugged Allegheny Mountains of West Virginia. Within the forest are areas of particular interest: Cranberry Glades, a bog forest likened to arctic tundra; Dolly Sods Scenic Area on Allegheny Mountain, noted for fall bird migration; Gaudineer Scenic Area, remnant of a virgin spruce forest; Seneca Rocks, a dramatic rock formation that towers over the surrounding terrain; and Spruce Knob, elevation 4,862 feet—the highest point in the state. Scenic drives, campgrounds, and 700 miles of hiking trails offer opportunities to see wildlife. *Best times to visit: spring, summer, and fall.*

Blackwater Falls State Park

Drawer 490
Davis, West Virginia 26260
telephone: (304) 259-5216

Located in the Potomac highlands of West Virginia, the state park includes the spectacular falls of the Blackwater River. Waters darkened with tannic acid from fallen spruce and hemlock needles tumble more than 50 feet, then pass through a gorge eight miles long. There are two major forest types in the 1,700-acre park: a northern coniferous forest of red spruce and fir and associated hemlock, and a northern hardwood forest of maple, beech, and birch. Several sphagnum bogs dot the park as well. An auto tour and ten miles of hiking and cross-country skiing trails offer opportunities to explore the area. Facilities include campgrounds, cabins, and a lodge. *Best time to visit: year-round.*

FOR FURTHER READING

Arora, David. *Mushrooms Demystified.* Berkeley: Ten Speed Press, 1987.

Barth, John. *The Sot-Weed Factor.* New York: Doubleday & Company, 1967.

Bartram, John. *John and William Bartram's America; selections from the writings of the Philadelphia naturalists.* Edited with an introduction by Helen Gere Cruickshank. New York: Devin-Adair, 1957.

Carter, Forrest. *The Education of Little Tree.* Albuquerque: University of New Mexico Press, 1989.

Eiseley, Loren. *The Immense Journey.* New York: Vintage Books, 1962.

Godfrey, Michael. *A Closer Look.* San Francisco: Sierra Club Books, 1975.

Godfrey, Michael. *A Sierra Club Naturalist's Guide to the Piedmont.* San Francisco: Sierra Club Books, 1980.

McPhee, John. *The Survival of the Bark Canoe.* New York: Farrar, Straus & Giroux, 1975.

Opler, Paul A., and George O. Krizek. *Butterflies East of the Great Plains, A Natural History.* Baltimore: Johns Hopkins University Press, 1984.

Pettingill, Olin Sewall, Jr. *A Guide to Bird Finding East of the Mississippi.* 2nd ed. New York: Oxford University Press, 1977.

Sams, Ferrol. *Run with the Horsemen.* Atlanta: Peachtree, 1982.

Sutton, Ann and Myron. *Eastern Forests.* New York: Alfred A. Knopf, 1987.

Terres, John K. *The Audubon Society Encyclopedia of North American Birds.* New York: Alfred A. Knopf, 1980.